4/11

P9-BVM-776

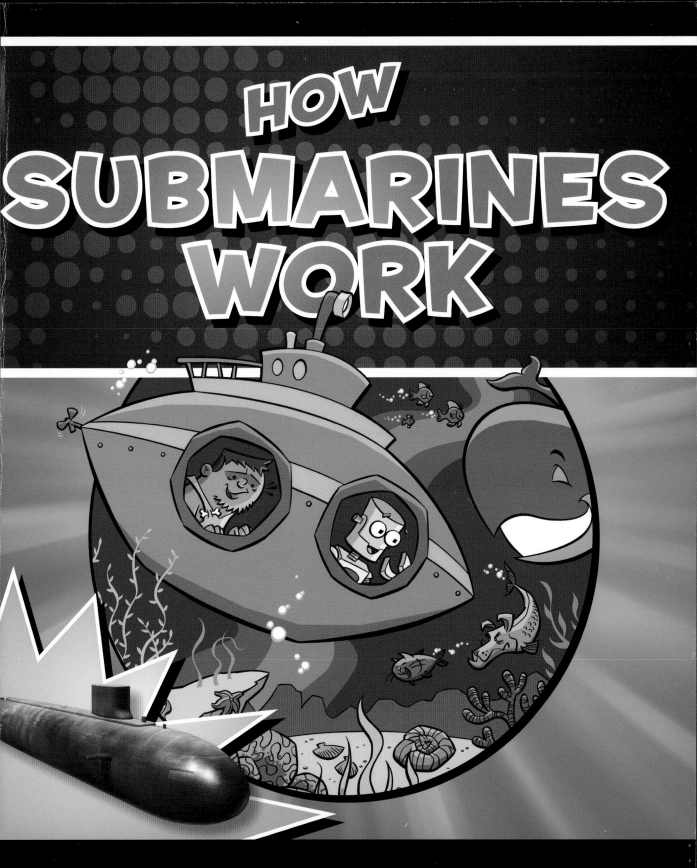

HOW SUBMARINES WORK

BY JENNIFER SWANSON • ILLUSTRATED BY GLEN MULLALY

Published by The Child's World®
1980 Lookout Drive • Mankato, MN 56003-1705
800-599-READ • www.childsworld.com

ACKNOWLEDGMENTS
The Child's World®: Mary Berendes, Publishing Director
Content Consultant: Paul Ohmann, PhD, Associate Professor
 of Physics, University of St. Thomas
The Design Lab: Design and production
Red Line Editorial: Editorial direction

LIBRARY OF CONGRESS
CATALOGING-IN-PUBLICATION DATA
Swanson, Jennifer.
  How submarines work / by Jennifer Swanson ;
illustrated by Glen Mullaly.
     p. cm.
  Includes bibliographical references and index.
  ISBN 978-1-60973-222-6 (library reinforced : alk. paper)
  1. Submarines (Ships)—Juvenile literature. I. Mullaly, Glen,
1968- ill. II. Title.
  V857.S93 2011
  623.825'7—dc23   2011013786

Photo Credits © Andrea Danti/Fotolia, cover, 1; Steven Wynn/
iStockphoto, 6, 20; Danna M. Morris/US Navy, 7; Andrew
McKaskle/US Navy, 9; Michael Watkins/iStockphoto, 10; Peter
Firus/iStockphoto, 15; Stefano Panzeri/Shutterstock Images,
17; Kevin Elliott/US Navy, 21 (top); Enrique Muller/Library of
Congress, 21 (bottom left); Library of Congress, 21 (bottom
right); J.Thompson/US Navy, 22; Ronald Gutridge/US Navy,
23 (top); Woods Hole Oceanographic Institutions/National
Oceanic and Atmospheric Administration, 23 (bottom);
Charles Grandin/US Navy, 29

Printed in the United States of America in Mankato,
Minnesota.
July 2011
PA02092

ABOUT THE AUTHOR
Jennifer Swanson's first love is science,
and she is thrilled to be able to combine
that with her passion for writing. She has
a bachelor of science in chemistry from
the US Naval Academy and a master of
science in education from Walden University.
Jennifer is currently employed as a middle
school science instructor for Johns Hopkins
University's Center for Talented Youth.

ABOUT THE ILLUSTRATOR
Glen Mullaly draws neato pictures for kids
of all ages from his swanky studio on the
west coast of Canada. He lives with his
awesomely understanding wife and their
spectacularly indifferent cat. Glen loves
old books, magazines, and cartoons, and
someday wants to illustrate a book on
How Monsters Work!

TABLE OF CONTENTS

CHAPTER ONE

SILENT CYLINDERS

Imagine yourself in a place where you can't tell night from day. You are cut off from phones, the Internet, television, and even radio—sometimes for months at a time. Do you know where you are?

You're underwater. Does that help?

"Dive! Dive! Dive!" The floor tilts down quickly, and you grab onto a chair to steady yourself. Do you know where you are now? A submarine, of course! Submarines are the silent ships of the deep. These long cylinders glide through ocean waters. They perform missions for the US Navy or collect data for scientific research.

How long have submarines been around? What did they look like 60, 150, 600, or even 2,000 years ago? Let's find out!

60 YEARS AGO

In 1954, the US Navy launched the *Nautilus*. This was the first submarine ever to be powered by a **nuclear reactor**. That important technology allowed the sub to stay underwater longer than ever before. It also meant the *Nautilus* could run very quietly, so enemies could not detect it.

150 YEARS AGO

In 1862, the *HL Hunley* was created by the Confederate States of America. This sub became the first to ever destroy an enemy warship in battle.

600 YEARS AGO

By now, Leonardo da Vinci had drawn the first sketches for a practical diving vessel. People were beginning to think about underwater travel.

2,000 YEARS AGO OR MORE

A legend states that Alexander the Great was able to travel underwater in a glass globe. But for the most part, voyages under the sea were simply not possible.

A 13th-century illustration of Alexander the Great's legendary underwater vessel

The US Navy keeps a fleet of about 71 submarines. Some of these warships are designed to attack enemy ships, while others can fire missiles at land targets. Submarines are effective warships because they operate underwater, where enemies cannot find them. US Navy submarines are also used to gather research, however. And smaller, scientific ships are taking ocean explorers deeper than ever before.

In the past, submarines had to come up for air every few hours. Both their crew and their engines needed a constant supply of oxygen. This made the submarines open to attack by enemies. Today, US Navy submarines can make their own air, and they have nuclear reactors. Their powerful engines do not require oxygen to run. These modern submarines can operate underwater for months at a time.

Crew members take in the view atop a floating submarine.

THE NUMBERS

How far down a submarine typically operates:
between 1,000 and 1,500 feet (305–457 m)

Deepest submarine dive on record: 35,813 feet (10,916 m)

Length of shortest US Navy submarine:
362 feet (110 m)—longer than one football field

Length of longest US Navy submarine: 560 feet (171 m)

Largest crew on a US Navy submarine: more than 150

COOL THINGS A SUB CAN DO

1. Keep control of the sea by making sure other ships stay where they are supposed to
2. Help get US Marines and US Navy SEALs to where they are needed
3. Help other ships in trouble
4. Lay mines in the ocean floor to prevent enemy ships from going through
5. Collect data on underwater creatures
6. Find sunken ships and treasure
7. Create underwater maps of the ocean
8. Measure the thickness of arctic ice to help scientists track global warming
9. Explore the deepest part of the ocean, where few humans have ever gone before

CHAPTER TWO

DOWN ... AND UP

Submarines can float on the surface. They can dive and glide through water without sinking to the bottom, and they can come back up. How does that work? To find out, you first have to understand density.

Everything in the world—from air to water to rocks—can be broken down into tiny pieces of matter called molecules. Molecules are so small, you'd need a very powerful microscope to see them.

Density tells you how tightly an object's molecules are packed together. Molecules that are far apart create low density, like in air. Tightly packed molecules create high density, like in a rock.

Whether something floats or sinks depends upon its density. In general, things that have a lower density than water float. Things that have a higher density than water sink.

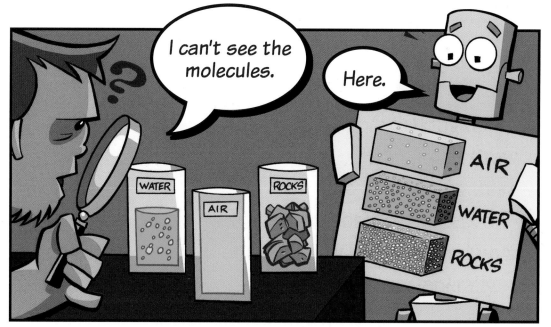

FILL 'ER UP

So how can a submarine both sink and float? Changing density is the key. This is done with the help of **ballast tanks**. These are metal tanks that can hold extra water from the sea. The tanks are located between the ship's outer and inner hulls, which are the frames and body of the sub. The tanks change the sub's density as they fill and empty with water.

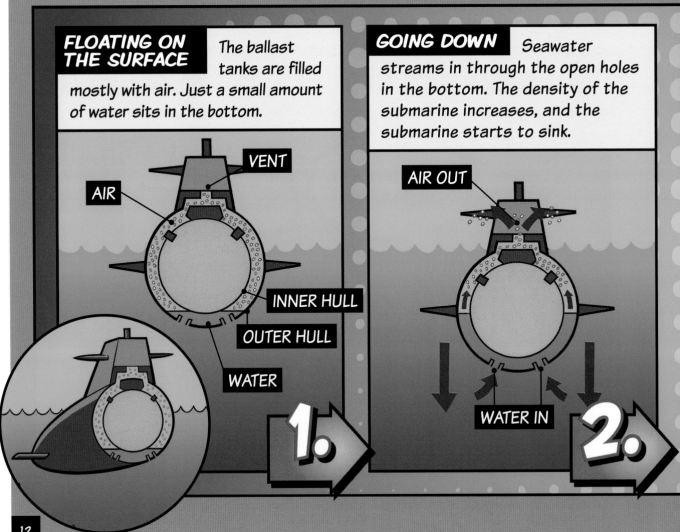

FLOATING ON THE SURFACE
The ballast tanks are filled mostly with air. Just a small amount of water sits in the bottom.

VENT
AIR
INNER HULL
OUTER HULL
WATER

1.

GOING DOWN
Seawater streams in through the open holes in the bottom. The density of the submarine increases, and the submarine starts to sink.

AIR OUT
WATER IN

2.

UP! NOW!

What if the submarine has to come up as fast as possible? That calls for an emergency blow. Air is forced quickly into the ballast tanks. The submarine shoots to the surface. It pops out of the water with a big splash.

UNDERWATER The tanks continue to fill with water. They close when the submarine's overall density is the same as the water around it. This way, the sub does not sink to the ocean floor.

3.

TIME TO GO UP The tanks open. Electric pumps force air into the tanks, pushing the water out of the open holes. The sub's density lowers, and the sub begins to rise.

4.

CHAPTER THREE

Underwater, a US Navy submarine can travel 29 miles per hour (47 km/h) or more. It takes a lot of power to push the giant craft through water. Where does that power come from?

FASTER!

A Look Inside the Engine Room

Today, a US Navy submarine never has to stop to fuel up. Its engine provides enough power for as long as the ship is in use.

How can this be? The answer comes down to two words: nuclear reactor. In it, there's a small supply of uranium, a heavy, silvery-white substance. This is the sub's fuel. But, unlike coal or oil, this fuel is not burned. Instead, it undergoes nuclear fission.

To understand *that*, you first have to understand atoms. Remember molecules? Well, atoms are even smaller. An atom is the most basic unit of matter. There are only 92 kinds of atoms in nature. Yet they combine to make up everything around us.

During nuclear fission, uranium atoms are split apart. This creates incredible heat.

Nuclear fission releases incredible amounts of energy.

LET'S SEE WHAT HAPPENS NEXT.

STEAM GENERATOR

NUCLEAR REACTOR

1. Pipes carry water from the steam generator to the nuclear reactor. Here, the water heats up. The hot water is kept under high pressure to keep it from boiling.

2. The high-pressure water goes back to the steam generator. This water gives off heat to boil other, regular water inside the generator, making steam.

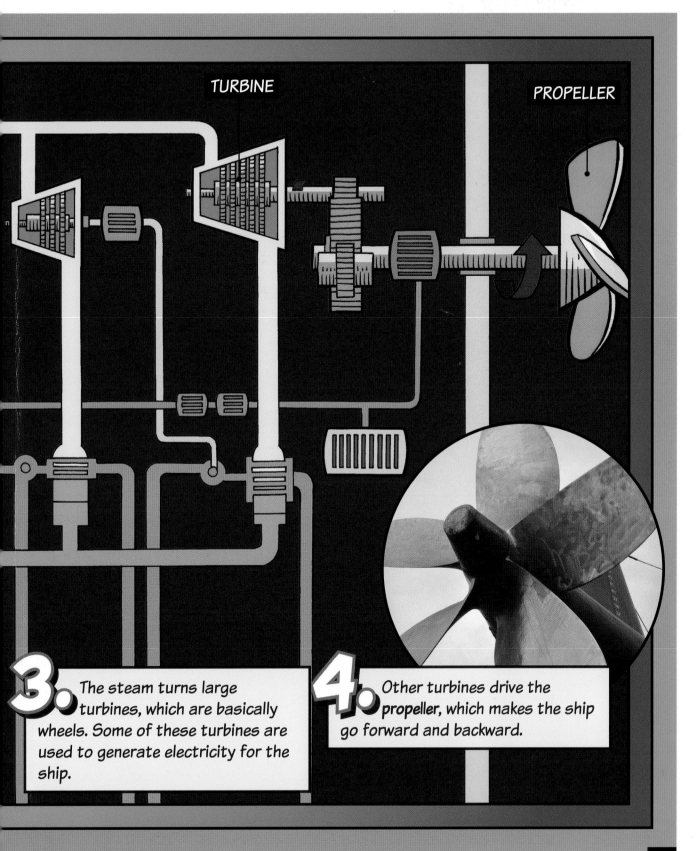

TURBINE

PROPELLER

3. The steam turns large turbines, which are basically wheels. Some of these turbines are used to generate electricity for the ship.

4. Other turbines drive the **propeller**, which makes the ship go forward and backward.

THE FIRST SUBMARINE

Cornelius van Drebbel, a Dutch doctor, built the first workable submarine around 1620. He made it out of a wooden rowboat that he covered with an oiled leather skin. Oars stuck out of the side, which the crew rowed by hand.

This sub was able to remain 15 feet (4.6 m) below sea level for several hours. The men aboard breathed through snorkels that stuck out the top of the leather skin. It's not hard to guess what this sub's downfall was—secrecy. Those snorkels sticking out of the water were a dead giveaway to anyone nearby.

CHAPTER FOUR

DON'T CRASH

When you are in a submarine, how do you know where you are going? Can you look out the front window like in a car? Well, no. A navy submarine doesn't have any windows at all. You may have ridden in a car that has a global positioning system, or GPS. This device has a screen that shows a map of where you are, and a computerized voice gives directions. GPS is helpful when the sub is on the surface, but it's unusable underwater. So, how do you drive a sub? Let's break it down.

How do you keep from getting lost?

You use something called **inertial guidance**. This system doesn't need any outside information. It doesn't send out radio waves, like radar does, or link to satellites, like a GPS. Instead, it tracks how the sub moves—how it speeds up, slows down, or changes direction. Based on this information (and some other stuff), a computer is constantly calculating where the submarine is. Imagine walking around your house wearing a blindfold. You could probably figure out where you were based on which way you went. That's kind of the same idea.

How do you keep from running into stuff?

Subs use **sonar** to "see" what's around them. Sonar sends out sound waves through the water. The waves hit

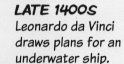

TIME LINE

AROUND 356 BC
As the story goes, Alexander the Great travels in a glass bulb under water.

LATE 1400S
Leonardo da Vinci draws plans for an underwater ship.

AROUND 1620
Cornelius van Drebbel makes the first practical submarine.

1776
The first known attack by a submarine takes place during the American Revolutionary War.

1800
The Nautilus becomes the first submarine to have a torpedo, or underwater missile.

Crew members are hard at work inside the control room of a US Navy submarine.

1864
HL Hunley is the first submarine to destroy an enemy ship.

1867
The first submarine with a steam-powered engine is built.

1900
The US Navy buys its first submarine, the USS Holland.

1902
The submarine **periscope** is invented.

1914–1918
German submarines called U-boats prove to be deadly weapons during World War I.

objects, including other ships, underwater mountains, whales, and more. Then the sound waves bounce back toward the sub. As they do, they scatter in interesting ways. The way those sound waves scatter can tell a lot about the thing they just hit—size, how far away it is, how fast it's moving, and what direction it's going. Computers analyze those sound waves to show what's around you.

What about steering?

For this, there's a steering wheel—just like the one in a car. Turning the wheel moves the **rudder**, a big, up-and-down fin on the back of the sub. This is used for moving right or left. Diving planes are sideways fins. They tilt to make the submarine go up and down. Push the steering wheel forward to go deeper; pull it toward you to go up.

1944
A US Navy submarine sinks a 71,890-ton (65,218-t) Japanese ship during World War II. That sets the record for the largest ship ever sunk by a submarine.

1954
The US Navy launches the *Nautilus*, the first nuclear-powered submarine.

1958
The *Nautilus* becomes the first submarine to explore under the North Pole's ice.

1960
The *Triton* becomes the first vessel to travel underwater around the world.

WHAT ABOUT THE PERISCOPE?

A periscope is a long tube in the submarine. The simplest kind has mirrors at both ends. You can look through the bottom and see out the top. A submarine's periscope can stretch up and poke out above the water. It provides a view of what's outside when the sub is within 60 feet (18 m) of the surface.

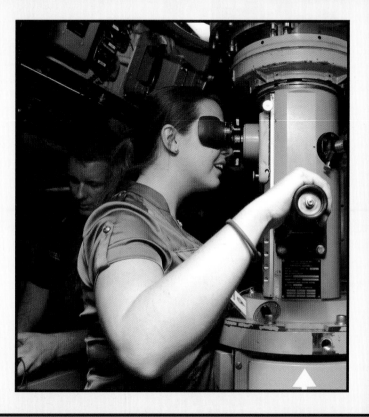

1964
Alvin becomes the first research submarine that can carry passengers.

1985
Remotely controlled **submersibles** find the wreckage of the *Titanic*, a famous passenger ship that sank in 1912.

2009
Robotic sub Nereus dives almost seven miles (11 km) to the deepest known part of any ocean, the Mariana Trench in the western Pacific Ocean.

2010
Women are allowed to serve on US Navy submarines.

Take a look inside a US Navy attack submarine. This smaller warship performs both military and scientific missions.

THE CREW OPERATES THE SUB FROM THE CONTROL ROOM

THE PERISCOPE IS FOR SEEING ABOVE WATER

THE TOP OF THE SAIL STICKS OUT OF THE WATER WHEN THE SUB IS TRAVELING ON THE SURFACE

THE CREW LIVES IN THE CREW'S QUARTERS

THE HULL IS MADE OF STEEL

BATTERIES STORE POWER FOR WHEN IT'S NEEDED

THE SONAR DOME IS FOR "SEEING" OBJECTS UNDERWATER

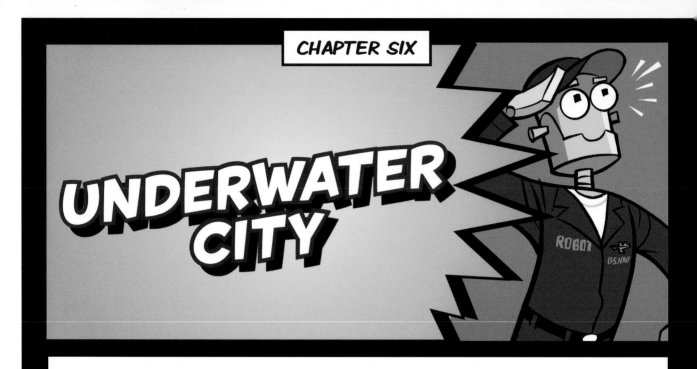

CHAPTER SIX

UNDERWATER CITY

A navy submarine serves as the crew's home for two to three months. Hundreds of meals a day are prepared in the submarine's kitchen. Crew members gather in the cafeteria, or mess hall, at mealtime. Libraries and game rooms are in the sub as well. Space is limited, so there's not much privacy. A single sleeping area may have up to 30 bunk beds. The crew works in shifts. When some are sleeping, others are working.

Gyms are found on all US Navy submarines. Exercise bikes, treadmills, and weights help keep a sailor physically fit. It is important to stay healthy when you're under the sea for so long.

A Day's Work

There are no sunrises or sunsets to rule days on a submarine. A typical day—the time from waking up one day to waking up the next—is 18 hours long. Crew members stand watch for six hours a day. During this time, they perform their assigned jobs. For the rest of the day, they are off-duty. They may eat, go to training classes, work out, read, or watch a movie. Generally, each sailor sleeps six hours during an 18-hour day.

LAUNDRY DUTY

Everyone onboard wears similar uniforms: one-piece blue coveralls and sneakers. The uniforms cut down on extra outfits, saving precious space. They save time, too. Just think how easy it would be to get dressed every morning. You wouldn't have to think about it at all.

Members of the crew are assigned to wash clothes and bedding in the sub's very own Laundromat. Each coverall has the owner's name on it. That way, each sailor is sure to get his or her own clothes back.

NO TEXTING

How do sailors stay in touch with their families back home? Letters and packages are picked up when the sub is docked and visiting cities. E-mail can be detected even underwater, so it is mostly off-limits. However, crew members are allowed to send e-mail during certain times.

The submarine has special equipment to send messages to US Navy people on land. On occasion, a sailor may be allowed to use this equipment to send news to a family member right away.

Sailors' family members wave good-bye to a departing US Navy submarine.

CHAPTER SEVEN

DEEPER AND DEEPER

Oceans cover two-thirds of our planet. And yet scientists guess that only a small portion—about 5 percent—of Earth's oceans has been explored. When it comes to oceans, humans really have only scratched the surface.

The *deep* refers to the part of the ocean below 18,000 feet (5,486 m). Here, thousands of species exist in some of the most extreme conditions on Earth. Miles of ocean water overhead make the water pressure crushing. No light reaches down this far. It is pitch black and extremely cold.

Small research subs called submersibles are the best way to explore the deep. Already, these subs have discovered ocean habitats and creatures. They have also revealed hints of valuable minerals and new fuel sources in the deep.

Some submersibles can carry small crews of two or three people. But most are unmanned. They are operated by people on ships, like remote-controlled toys. Many submersibles are robotic and have built-in computers that tell them what to do.

These subs are making amazing discoveries, and yet they could do so much more. Scientists are looking for ways to make them both stronger and lighter. They need better lights to shine into the deep. These subs are battery-operated, and they need better batteries so they can stay underwater longer.

Scientists are also looking for ways to make submersibles better "swimmers." Their goal? Submarines that move as freely through the ocean as the animals that live there.

WORDS TO KNOW

ballast tanks (BAL-uhst TANGKZ): Ballast tanks are compartments in a submarine that hold seawater. Ballast tanks fill and empty to allow the submarine to dive or surface.

inertial guidance (ihn-UR-shuhl GY-duhns): A submarine uses inertial guidance to figure out its position underwater. With inertial guidance, a sub uses data about its own motion instead of radio waves, satellites, or any other outside source of information.

nuclear reactor (NOO-klee-uhr ree-AK-tuhr): A nuclear reactor creates incredible heat by splitting apart uranium atoms. Today, a US Navy sub is powered by a nuclear reactor.

periscope (PEHR-uh-skohp): A periscope is a long tube that provides a view of the surface for crew members inside a submarine. A periscope is only usable when the submarine is close to the surface, however.

propeller (pruh-PEHL-uhr): A propeller looks like a fan at the back end of a submarine. The propeller spins to drive the submarine backward or forward.

rudder (RUHD-uhr): A rudder is a sideways fin at the back of a submarine. The rudder is tilted to move the submarine left or right.

sonar (SOH-nahr): Sonar is the system that allows people onboard a submarine to know what objects are in the surrounding ocean. Sonar works by sending out sound waves that can be analyzed by computers.

submersibles (suhb-MUR-suh-buhls): Submersibles are small, research submarines. Submersibles are the best way to study the deepest parts of oceans.

INDEX

FIND OUT MORE

Visit our Web site for links about how submarines work: childsworld.com/links

Note to Parents, Teachers, and Librarians: We routinely verify our Web links to make sure they are safe and active sites. So encourage your readers to check them out!